NISSAN MOTOR CORPORATION
U.S.A.

Dear Adventure Lover:

Warren Miller has been chasing the world's best skiers down the world's best mountains—and recording it all on film—for 47 years. In *Ski Fever*, a photographic account of these breathtaking adventures, it's more of the same.

Just as on the big screen, the pages of this book are a heart-pounding rush. Whether you're an adventurer, or just an adventurer-at-heart, Miller's images will get your adrenaline flowing.

We are proud to be part of Warren Miller's on-going quest for the perfect lung-burning, thigh-screaming, wind-in-your-face ski run. Our Pathfinder fits right in. In fact, the 1996 Nissan® Pathfinder® is both the "official vehicle" and the "official sponsor" of Miller's latest film, *Endless Winter*.

This arrangement was not just in name only. The *Endless Winter* crew relied on the Pathfinder in extreme situations on remote locations around the world during filming. It came through with flying colors.

With its rugged good looks and shift-on-the-fly 4WD, it's a sport-utility vehicle that invites you to go anywhere, anytime—and it's particularly well-suited for cold weather where comfort and dependability are requisite qualities.

It's a perfect match, Warren Miller and the Nissan Pathfinder. Both promise adventure and the dream of freedom without boundaries. And both deliver.

Whether or not you get your thrills flying down icy mountainsides, we at Nissan hope you'll enjoy *Ski Fever*, and that it will motivate and inspire the adventurous spirit in you.

Sincerely,

Earl J. Hesterberg
Vice President
General Manager, Nissan Division

It's time to expect more from a car.

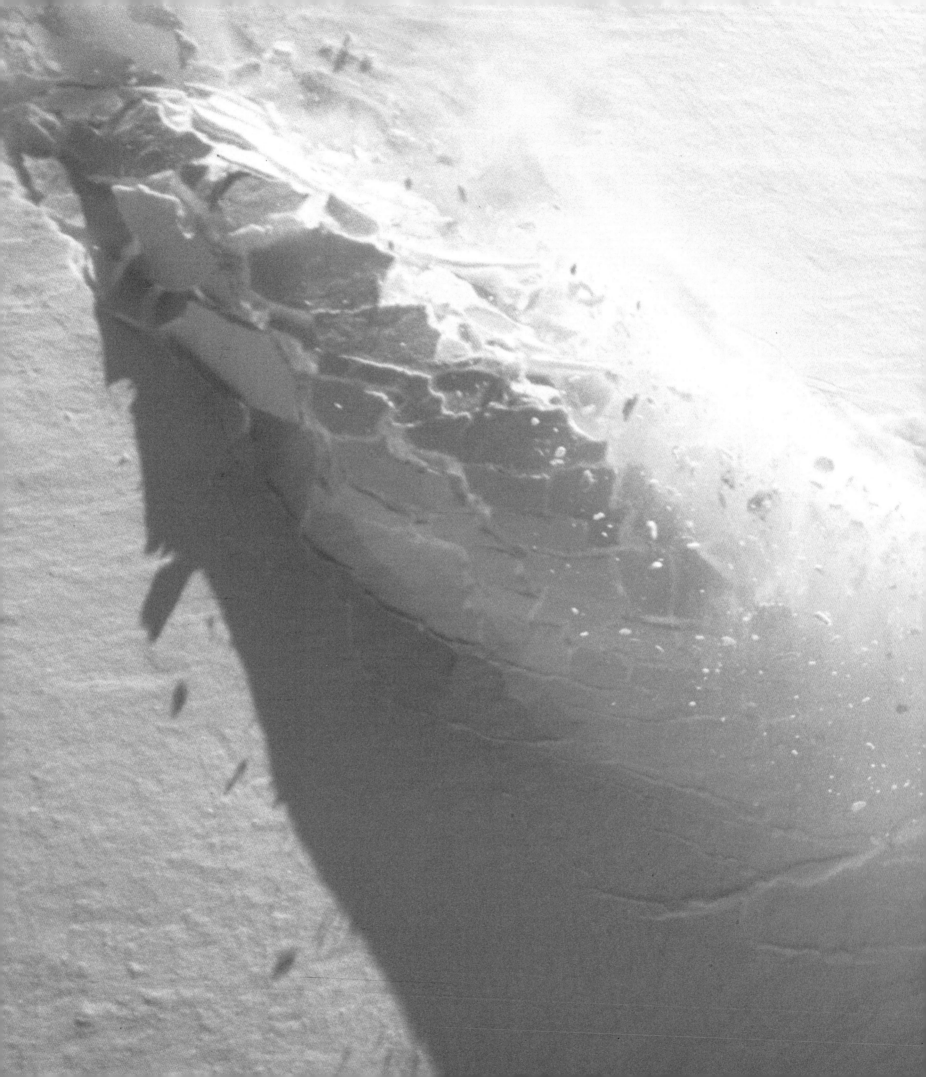

Warren Miller's
SkiFever!

TEHABI BOOKS
DEL MAR, CALIFORNIA

Warren Miller's Ski Fever! was conceived and produced by Tehabi Books, Del Mar, California.
Nancy Cash–*Managing Editor*; Andy Lewis–*Project Art Director*; Sam Lewis–*Art Director*;
Tom Lewis–*Editorial and Design Director*; Sharon Lewis–*Controller*; Chris Capen–*President*.
Additional support for *Ski Fever!* was also provided by Laura Georgakakos–*Copy Editor* and
Marla Markman–*Copy Proofer*.

For additional copies of this book, corporate customized editions or more information please
contact: Chris Capen, Tehabi Books, 13070 Via Grimaldi, Del Mar, California, 92014, 619/481-7600.

Tehabi Books, in association with The Basic Foundation, a not-for-profit organization whose
primary mission is reforestation, will facilitate the planting of two trees for every one tree used in the
manufacture of this book.

Library of Congress Cataloging-in-Publication Data
   Ski Fever!
     Warren Miller's Ski Fever! / [edited by Richard Needham, with preface by Warren Miller].
   -- 1st ed.
       p.   cm.
     Collection of essays about skiing.
     ISBN 1-887656-00-6 (hardcover)
     ISBN 0-06-258662-9 (softcover)
     1. Skis and skiing--Miscellanea. I. Miller, Warren, film writer. II. Needham, Richard,
   1939- .   III. Title.
   GV854.S5824 1995
   796.93--dc20   95-30876
                                                    CIP

95 96 97 98 TBI 10 9 8 7 6 5 4 3 1

This edition is printed on acid-free paper that meets the American National Standards Institute
Z39.48 Standard.

Printed in Hong Kong through Mandarin Offset.

Warren Miller's
SkiFever!

BY WARREN MILLER

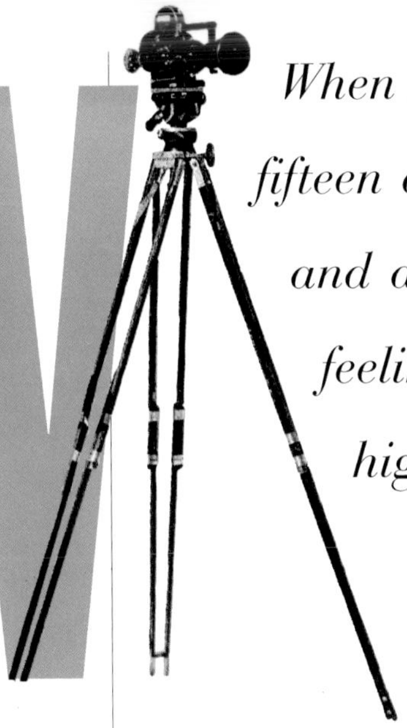

When I started showing my ski films in 1950, there were fewer than fifteen chairlifts in North America. That was almost fifty years ago and a lot has changed in skiing since then. But not the pure gut feeling of making a turn on the side of a hill with one foot a little higher than the other.

For many years, I traveled all over the world while I filmed, wrote, edited, scored, booked, and narrated each ski film showing.

One year, after traveling to 108 cities to show and narrate the feature ski film and after sleeping in 212 different hotels, a friend told me that I could put my voice right on the sound track. It was then that I discovered that other people could do some of the work I had been doing and, sometimes, do it better.

SkiRuns, SkiReels

THROUGH THE ARLBERG PASS WITH SKIS AND A CAMERA

"Anyone who tells you that they can ski as well at fifty years of age as they could when they were twenty wasn't very good when they were twenty."

—Warren Miller

So I hired a secretary, then a cameraman, a couple of years later a salesman, then a part-time film editor, and finally a production manager. As my three children grew up, two of my children went their own way and started their own businesses. My youngest son, Kurt, went to work full time for me. That was after he had won All-American honors three times in college as a sailor.

By then I had a full-time staff of almost a dozen people. Over the years Kurt learned the film business and eventually bought it from me.

Now at my senior-citizen age of seventy, all of the filmmaking decisions are in others hands. It's my time to watch the snow reports and ski in powder snow without a fifty-pound rucksack full of cameras and a weather map and watch everyone else do all of the work instead. A full-time crew of sixteen people now produces the movies. I simply write the scripts and narrate them after they are shot and edited.

As I look forward to the next thirty years, it's gratifying to see the Warren Miller film genre continue to grow under the guidance of my son Kurt and his partner, Peter Speek.

As long as it continues to be fun to ski and write scripts, I will continue to contribute to that film genre. In the meantime, this book—the best work of contemporary still photographers and skiing's leading writers—is a literary-visual treat reflecting the variety and pace of the sport of skiing.

It is a true testimony to the fact that you can only do four things on skis. You can turn right, you can turn left, you can go straight, or you can sell them. There's a good chance you will find me doing the first three for a long time to come.

Warren Miller and Mount Snow personality Rudi Wyrsch (opposite) discuss the filming of a scene in 1972.

BY RICHARD NEEDHAM

There are two kinds of fever. There's the ugly, I-think-I've-bought-the-farm kind. The kind you suffer after you get bitten by a deer tick and start thinking about calling Aunt Mary about that falling-out fifteen years ago and then start rewriting your will.

That's the bad kind.

Then there's the ecstatic, trance-inducing, double whammy I-think-I've-just-been-goosed kind. The kind that tickles your nerve endings, redlines your juices, and just sends you soaring.

That's the good—the best—kind.

And that's the kind of fever this book is about: the crazy, who-knows-why addiction of a sport—a lifestyle, if you're more comfortable with that—that consumes our passion, our conversation, our relationships, our zeitgeist, like no other.

It's really insidious when you think about it. Skiing is a drug, an emotional and physical and spiritual hit that grabs you with such unyielding and unshakable force that when you're deprived of your daily, weekend, or seasonal dose, it makes you absolute hell to live with.

SkiTime
THE ADDICTIVE POWER OF THE SPORT

I'd like to say that I contracted my own ski fever while pushing off down a mountain mantled in white, whiffing the sweet aroma of klister and wood smoke, hearing the squeak of snow underfoot, and making a perfectly carved turn.

But it didn't happen that way. What I saw were a steady stream of interstate headlights, what I whiffed were the fumes from a busted radiator hose, and what I made were bathtub-sized craters—or sitzmarks, as they were more properly called—the length of the slope.

I blame my brother. He got the good stuff—skates, pads, gloves, all the paraphernalia a kid needs for a boarding school hockey career. What I got were his too-long (I was six years younger than he was) Northland ridge-top hickory skis with cable bindings, rickety bamboo poles with no grips, and Mickey Mouse (aptly named if you remember them) warped leather boots.

* * *

In 1958, I was one of five midwestern college guys who had just seen and been gassed by Warren Miller's, "Are Your Skis On Straight?" and we were heading north to Caberfae, Michigan, for our first experience on skis. Skiing, of course, wasn't the class act that it is today. But neither were we. Oggies' '47 Packard sprang a radiator leak, which necessitated our buying several cases of Buckeye beer—*faux* antifreeze that we kept pouring into Oggie's wheezing engine block. Since the Buckeye didn't taste a whole lot better than antifreeze, we weren't too upset about giving our ration to the radiator.

Fifteen hours later, as the sun was coming up, Oggie's Packard with the beer breath deposited us in the Caberfae parking lot. Since none of us had skied before, our first moves were touch-and-go. Make that crawl-and-fall. But we watched other skiers make their swooping, elegant, knees-welded turns and tried to copy what they did. It wasn't easy, given my brother's hand-me-down gear.

Then it happened. Two perfectly linked turns. Okay, make that two turns—one just before lunch; the other just after. No matter, I was hooked. Unequivocally, irretrievably, indisputably, positively, absolutely hooked.

"It really doesn't matter whether you ski at a resort, poke around the puckerbrush, get goofy in powder, race, board, or stretch your gut on the extreme. Skiing has the adaptability to mold into whatever experience you want it to be."

What happened that first day on skis was: I got The Fever. I started memorizing cool Austrian phrases like *wedeln, gegenschulter, gelandesprung, gemutlichkeit and gluhwein.* I also became a gear geek. That day at Caberfae, having observed that most skiers were skiing on black skis (they were, I was later to find out, metal Head Standards), I got a bucket of black paint when I got home and, presto, instantly transformed my boards into very impressive high-tech stuff. I really didn't fool anybody—the snickers in the lift line told me that, but at least I felt I was part of this whole marvelous, wonderful, energizing scene.

* * *

By 1964, I was so into skiing, so smitten by The Fever, that I joined a ski club. Every week we would meet and listen to tales of exotic trips to places like Utah and Colorado while we oohed and aahed over dog-eared photos. And every weekend we'd head for our barn-cum-ski-house in Rochester, Vermont, to enjoy our private little quarantine for sufferers of the Fever. It was a cocoon, really; a warm, cozy den of like-minded denizens who talked nonstop and late into the night about skiing—great runs of the day, neat off-trail and *aprés*-ski discoveries. And isn't it nice to have a nest with a roaring fire, wet wool socks on the hearth, seedy overstuffed chairs, warm bunks, and the camaraderie of other inmates serving their weekend parole together?

If all this sounds wonderfully nostalgic, there were down moments, too. Like The Hangover. If you didn't have one the morning after the night you arrived, you just weren't considered serious about this ski thing. And the chores. If you forgot to tend to what you signed up to do on the weekend sleep-and-weep sheet (buy the food, start the furnace, stoke the fire, clean the bathrooms, cook Sunday breakfast), you forfeited your bunk the next weekend.

* * *

By 1974, there were three little skiers in the Needham household, all born, to my non-skiing in-laws' angst, with the same genetic defect: *skiagrobundinitis.* The Fever.

Most kids look forward to summer. Not mine. They clomped around in their tiny ski boots beginning with the leaves' first fall. They practiced their pole plants on the living room carpet. They wore their goggles to school. They, like Dad, had The Fever—fueled by evenings at Stratton Mountain's Birkenhaus, where they gathered in front of the fire in their sleepers to listen

You don't have to be a Baryshnikov to do it. All you need is a touch of Eddy the Eagle, of subliminal need to break away from the humdrum and life's mind-strangling preoccupations, and just go dance on the mountain.

to Emo Heinrich's stirring accounts of great avalanche rescues, mountaineering adventures, and lessons on how to yodel while slurping the last of their *strudl mit schlag.*

By this time, I had completely given in to my addiction—I'd tried helicopter skiing, backcountry skiing, snowcat skiing, even hang-gliding on skis—and had taken the ultimate leap. I started a sort of pen-pal relationship with others similarly afflicted and became editor of *SKI Magazine.* Now I could prophesy, soothsay, preach, inculcate and indoctrinate to my heart's content. If I've got The Fever, I figured modestly, I'm going to take the whole damn world with me.

Along the way, I met others who had the rare gift of being able to talk frankly and openly about their "problem." And you'll hear from these hapless souls in the pages that follow.

What they have to tell you—what I will tell you—is that it really doesn't matter whether you ski at a resort, poke around the puckerbrush, get goofy in powder, race, board, or stretch your gut in the extreme. Skiing has this wonderful adaptability to meld into whatever experience you want it to be.

I can smell the wood smoke now, and the klister, and the waxing iron, and I can hear the crackle of a fire and the squeak of snow crystals underfoot. Can't you? ✎

"Then it happened. Two perfectly linked turns. Okay, make that two turns—one just before lunch; the other just after. No matter, I was hooked. Unequivocally, irretrievably, indisputably, positively, absolutely hooked."

Snow comes in many forms, and it has many names. Eskimos call it Annui, Api, Qali, Pukak, Siqoq or, depending on its form and consistency, any of thirty-two other names. But to a skier there's only one word—powder—and it conjures up sexy, emotional, magical images. To the powder pig who won't ski anything else, it's better than anything else. Period. To skiers who know the sensual, body-hugging feeling of whispery soft, almost nonsnow snow, it's mecca, the ultimate high.

Remember those pillow fights you had as a kid when all those light, white floaty feathers showered the room, and how it felt to fall in them? Powder is like that. Skiers who have never experienced powder fancy themselves carving big rooster-tail turns, contrails cascading from their body as they apply their brushstrokes to the terrain and porpoise down the mountain.

It's like that.

PowderBlasts
SKIING THE DEEP—AT ITS BEST

THE VOICE OF NEW SNOW

BY PETER OLIVER

Droplets of ordinary water, formed in the atmosphere around microscopic specks of matter and bonded in the deep freeze of wintertime air. When reduced to its basic elements, snow is piddling, uncomplicated stuff: water, dust, and air.

How astonishing it is then, that this humble mix can transform the world. It sneaks out of the sky and sifts onto mountainsides to redefine the shape and contour of the land. It plays games with color and contrast and traps sunlight on its surface in jewels of refracted energy. It attaches as filigree to the slenderest of tree branches in a nimble display of lightness and balance. Air is about ninety percent of the mixture—when you scoop up a handful of fresh snow and blow at it, it disappears into puffs swirling away to nowhere.

This all seems like magic to me—filigree and jewels made from dust, water, and air. So I suppose it's also magic that this same mix of dust and water and air can provide the absolute best time a person can have outdoors in winter. I'm talking, of course, about powder skiing.

Powder skiing can do the most peculiar things to your senses and sensibilities, and it has been my good luck to have had a fair amount of experience with it. I have skied in powder deep enough to blind and choke me as it arcs upward from the tips of my skis. I have skied in the kind of dense powder that compresses like a spring-loaded mattress beneath my skis, expelling me at the finish of each turn into a heady millisecond of zero gravity. I have skied in powder that hisses against my edges, that squeaks with coldness, that groans as layers of the snowpack settle. It can talk, by God! Making noises like that, powder can fool you into thinking that it is a living thing.

* * *

It was a cold, gray day among the charred remnants of a once-impressive forest of fir and spruce. Two feet of new snow had already fallen in the Cariboo Mountains of British Columbia, and the dull color of the sky indicated that more snow was on the way. Six of us were skiing in that burned forest where the snow lay stable and undisturbed by wind. It would have been dangerous to go higher in the mountains, above the tree line into

It requires a different technique? Yes. It requires finesse. It requires a sensitivity to the elements and an awareness of your body in space. And it requires that you loosen up, that you unlearn that hard-edge, body-contorting, beat-the-mountain-into-submission mentality. It is worth it. Just ask any powder skier.

the cirques and couloirs and open bowls. In those big open spaces, the new snow had formed a deep and beguiling layer that tried to sucker us in with its soft, gentle appearance. It was a death trap, and we knew it. Unless you've witnessed an avalanche, it's hard to fathom that this same insubstantial airy stuff, able to be blown away with a simple breath, has the power to engulf and crush you.

Down in the burn where it was safe, I was skiing along the backbone of a whaleback ridge, taking immense pleasure in the feeling of snow washing over my shoulders and gathering coldly in the space between my neck and coat collar. I stopped to survey my surroundings, to soak in the somber beauty of a burned forest on a snowy day.

I watched a skier in a gully below me navigate through the maze of black trees. He was ripping—fast, energetic, and a little bit reckless. The air was still enough that I could hear the snow splashing softly against his chest with each turn and hear his noises of pleasure.

As he executed one particularly emphatic turn, a bird flew up from the snow near his ski tips in a panicked escape from the sudden intrusion. It was a ptarmigan, whose summer-brown feathers turn white in winter as a seasonal disguise to divert predators. The unsuspecting bird, perhaps napping in the new snow, flew up and out of the burn, its wings making a kind of purring sound. It flew up through the blackened spears of former trees trying to lose itself in the curtain of snowfall. Skiing in a black forest on a cold winter day filled with the sounds and sensations and deadly lure of fresh powder—and a white bird rises out of the snow.

It was over in seconds—the bird was gone, and the skier skied on. I went back to skiing too, feeling the cold gathering inside my collar and listening to the snow as it talked to me, laying down fresh tracks on the new contours of a world redefined by a fresh snowfall. Powder skiing. ✖

SKI FEVER!

LOCAL POWDER

BY DAVID GOODMAN

The snowstorm raging outside spat a tornado of snow in behind me. "Welcome home," said my wife, Sue, as I came through the door. "Hope you still have a few turns left. Over a foot by tomorrow morning—maybe two," she said, beaming. I managed to muster a weak smile.

It wasn't that I was unenthused about the promise of a powder day. It's just that I was fresh off a week of helicopter skiing in British Columbia. And, as my heli-ski partners were prone to repeat in a glassy-eyed daze, it doesn't get any better than that. I was exhausted when I got home. Would I ever experience snow and skiing like that again?

But even with an ecstasy hangover, I was instinctively excited by the forecast at home. Local powder is different from powder anywhere else. A big dump on your home turf is a community event. Daily routines stop and everyone you know is focused on one thing: snow. For some, it's just the hassle of digging out, but for others it's inspiration to plunge into the white stuff in any kind of vehicle, from sleds and inner tubes to skis and snowboards. What makes a powder day at home better than anywhere else isn't just the snow, it's the people. You're joined in your passions by neighbors, friends, and family. And later, at home, powder days will be just as enjoyable in the retelling.

The following morning, Sue and I struggled through gusting winds, drifted roads, and eighteen inches of new snow to get to the base of our local hill. We've gotten to know this craggy, majestic mountain intimately over the years, thrilling to every nuance we stumble upon, mining each new powder trove for turns. There are many rewards for skiers involved in these explorations. You learn where to look for untapped treasures. Knowing how the wind blows across a ridge offers clues to where you might find an overlooked powder shot. And a feeling for how the sun moves around the mountain allows you to move with it. So while the neophytes are skiing sunbaked muck, you're still ripping powder in the shadows.

In the chairlift, we studied how the storm had worked the mountain. The wind had played its usual tricks, burying some trails in powder, leaving only wisps of white on others. Our eyes wandered over to the historic double-diamond test pieces of the mountain. The top of one, a steep headwall that is usually a minefield of moguls, was submerged in white.

"**K**nowing how the wind blows across a ridge offers clues to where you might find an overlooked powder shot. And a feeling for how the sun moves around the mountain allows you to move with it."

We quickly made our way to the trail, where we were met by an old friend, a carpenter who had been teaching and skiing here for over twenty years. "Hope B.C. didn't ruin your taste for local powder," said Dudley with a grin as he pushed off then disappeared over the lip. Sue and I dropped in on his heels.

My skis and lower legs vanished in the fluff. With gravity's help, I burst up out of the snow and dropped into my next turn. Suddenly, a sharp cold smack hit me in the jaw; a face shot on the first turn was a warning that this was no ordinary run. I shot out of the snowdrift and flew about five feet through the air. A rooster tail of cold smoke trailed me as I landed in an even deeper trough. White foam erupted around my waist then exploded in chaos around my head. My mouth, wide open as I gasped with pleasure and surprise on each landing, suddenly filled with snow. I couldn't breathe, but I was still moving faster and faster, unable to see beyond the white haze. One turn later, I managed to spit out the powdery plug, suck in a huge gulp of air, and ski out of my private blizzard. I let out an involuntary, raspy yelp before torpedoing through another four-foot-deep powder pile. Within seconds, my mouth filled with snow again as yet another cold wave boiled up and submerged me. I coughed and spat while my skis surfaced and dove down the fall line like playful porpoises, rhythmically launching into the air out of each turn and landing in deeper furrows of sugar. Snow poured down my collar, billowed over my head, washed under my arms. Again I gasped for air; again my mouth filled with snow. Going too fast…can't stop…too much snow…too much air…flying.

I came to a halt near Dudley. Both of us were doubled over, chests heaving like land-locked fish and smiling numbly. I looked up to see Sue still skiing, alternately launching through the air and exploding through powder in a perfect fall line waltz. Her dance was punctuated by rhythmic hoots of delight as snow swirled around her in exuberant accompaniment.

I stood on the slope, dumbstruck. It wasn't as if I hadn't seen snow all year—after all, I had just come from a powder paradise. But turn after turn of choking face shots? Never in my life. Not in Jackson, Alta, Vail, or even in B.C. This was an epic run, unmatched by anything I'd ever skied in my travels.

I shouldn't have been surprised. There's great skiing and deep powder in far-flung mountain ranges. But to find buried treasure, you have to come home. ⛷

PUSH AND PUNCH IN THE DEEP

BY LITO TEJADA-FLORES

While expert skiers unanimously agree that skiing powder is easier than skiing on the pack, many skiers aren't so sure. It seems one has to cross a "powder threshold" to really do it, to believe in it. Technically, that threshold involves weighting both skis equally because unequally weighted skis tend to separate—one dives, one floats, and you fall. But equally weighted skis float equally in the deep, and here's a trick to make it happen.

It's hard to stand equally balanced on both feet, both skis. It's much easier to move both feet together. In this case, equal action means equal weighting means equal flotation which, in powder, means happiness. And the action to concentrate on is this: At the start of your powder turn, push the toes of both boots forward and down the hill. Let me say it again, differently: push both feet forward into the new turn.

Sound funny? I know it does. In fact, you can hardly push your feet forward at all. But it's the effort of trying to do so that guarantees that both skis will be equally weighted and will turn together in powder. It works.

Another tip: In deeper or heavier powder, punch your outside hand and pole straight up as you start to turn. I'm talking about lifting your right hand, suddenly and rapidly, as you launch a turn to the left, and vice versa. Why? This simple gesture is a classic powder skier's trick. It achieves what I call differential unweighting—not just helping you lighten your skis but taking more weight off the tips than the tails—and it also banks you strongly into the turn so that your ski bases, also banked over, are pushed into the new turn by the resistance of the powder against them.

Finally, a more recent powder skier's trick: Rent or buy a pair of fat powder skis. These wide, short skis are not a gimmick or passing fad. In fact, they work wonders, especially for skiers inexperienced in the deep. Fat powder skis provide much more flotation in deep snow. As a result, weighting both skis equally, while still a good idea, becomes less critical. If you do get off on one ski you won't crash, because that one fat ski has about as much flotation as two normal skis do. There's no learning curve on these skis. You step in, push off, and it works. Fat skis are a great tool even for expert skiers—they make breakable crust feel like friendly powder. And for skiers who have never considered powder friendly, they are a revelation. ✨

"In deeper or heavier powder, punch your outside hand and pole straight up as you start to turn....This simple gesture is a classic powder skier's trick."

We've all had our rush in skiing. For some, it's that first no-fall turn. For others, it's skiing that menacing black diamond and arriving at the bottom with all body parts intact. For others— very few others—it's the gut-wrenching, thigh-pounding, nerve-exploding experience of redlining it down a mountain at sixty miles per hour plus. Knowing that the surface below you is ice. Knowing that even the slightest mistake—or fogged goggle or dinged edge—can cost you your life.

It's called downhill. It's done by the world's best skiers, and it's done by college skiers and by skiers not yet in their teens. The courses may be different—shorter, longer, steeper, flatter—but the apprehensions and the why-am-I-here seldom change.

And neither does the rush.

WhataRush!

THE THRILLS AND CHILLS OF HIGH-OCTANE SKIING

HELL BREAKS LOOSE
by Paul Hochman

ALWAYS DOWNHILL, ALWAYS FASTER
by Charlie Meyers

HELL BREAKS LOOSE

BY PAUL HOCHMAN

Speed hangs like an opium cloud over the start corral at a downhill. I can see it in the down-turned faces and averted eyes of my fellow helmeted, skin-suited junkies. And I can see it in the furtive tinkerings of the suppliers, the equipment jocks who kneel around us and ply us with paraphernalia—the drills, the drivers, the liquid waxes—and prepare us as best they can for the wild trip down.

"The first thing you'll feel when you get going fast is your hands," said Bart, my first downhill coach. "You'll be gripping your poles too tight." He was preparing us for the body's natural urge to get as much speed as it can, while the mind simultaneously tries to get the body to listen to reason. "Because, after all," he told us, "eighty miles per hour is not a natural act." We all laugh nervously. "So," said Bart, "when you get into the start house and you can feel the sweat and you can hear your heartbeat echoing off the walls, just think about relaxing your hands."

So there I was, in the start house of my first downhill, looking at the parking lot three miles below me, looking at the sun reflecting off the blue ice in the first turn—in short, thinking about everything but my hands. In the start corral the craziness was beginning. One racer sank down to his knees, eyes closed, hands out in front of him. He looked like he was praying but, actually, his hands were running the race; fingers leapt out of the start house, hung on through the first big turn, glided weightlessly over the rock-hard flats, and then dropped fast onto the headwall. It's a pantomime played out by racers all over the world, a miniature theatrical event designed to inspire them to ski so fast that their hair catches fire.

"When you go over that first headwall," Bart tells me, "that's when you'll feel it first. If you notice that your toes are clenched, think back to your hands. They probably got tense first. Remember, a lot of the tension is a natural response to the sound of the wind. Block it out." But it's hard to block it out. As I drop out of the start house, the roar in my ears begins at about thirty miles per hour and grows exponentially from there. At eighty, I'm sure my ears are going to explode. But that's nothing compared to what it sounds like to spectators.

"You understand the real speed of downhill skiing when you discover that the Doppler effect applies to your own plummeting body as much as it does to speeding freight trains and exploding galaxies."

In a downhill, the racers are audible before they are visible. The skier's body creates a telltale whoosh as it pushes the air in front of it. In fact, downhillers sound roughly like Indy cars do, only there are no exhaust fumes. When the racer finally appears, head down, clenched into a muscular ball, the frequency of the sound rises. It rises further as the racer's body rockets downward toward the spectators and jams the air into increasingly tighter spaces. The noise reaches its height at the moment the racer passes by and then it drops quickly, like the siren on a police car speeding to a murder scene.

If someone tells you that the way to duplicate the feeling of dropping off a headwall in a downhill is to put on a bike helmet and stick your head out of a car window, they've left out a few details. For one thing, in a car it doesn't feel like you're being shaken like a leaf in a hurricane. And it doesn't feel like somebody's beating you with a stick. A closer approximation of the feeling of a downhill would be to jump up and down on the top of a car going eighty miles per hour....on a dirt road.

From the outside, it all looks so deceptively smooth, and that's the beginning of the thrill—you can see me laying my ski out there a meter from my body, setting up a platform over my thighs and riding my skis like they were train rails. But inside my helmet, all hell is breaking loose. The wind is so loud I can't think straight. The tiny undulations and dings left in the snow by previous racers that look innocent from the living room couch are, in fact, rattling my fillings. And my goggles, no matter how tightly strapped to my face, are shaking so hard with each bump that what is in front of me is an educated guess. I struggle to stay in my tuck as the spruce trees become a blur.

"Focus ahead of you," Bart said, "because where you are has already gone by." It's a philosophy for the ages, and it's where the thrill begins to make sense, to take on substance. Because it is at the highest speeds that, for a few transcendent moments, things slow down. It's like Chuck Yaeger's experience breaking the sound barrier for the first time. As he approached Mach I, Yaeger's jet began to shake so hard that he considered backing off on the stick. Then he pushed it forward. On the ground, when they heard the boom, the technicians were sure the jet had exploded. In the air, Yaeger experienced the opposite sensation. It was as if the jet had

"There are moments when the wind roars so loudly, it is no longer audible; the shaking suddenly goes away; the tips, which for so many seconds seemed ready to vibrate apart, suddenly track and glide like skates on ice."

disappeared and had left him up there, hurtling quietly through space at 700 miles per hour. Speed-rendered calm.

It is the same on a pair of downhill skis. There are moments when the wind roars so loudly, it is no longer audible; the shaking suddenly goes away; the tips, which for so many seconds seemed ready to vibrate apart, suddenly track and glide like skates on ice. It may be that the brain can only process so much information so quickly, and all that's left is sight and feel. And it may be that Einstein was right: At higher speeds, time does slow down.

It's quiet at the top of the race hill on the morning of a downhill. All those racers are just waiting for their turn to stop Father Time, to defy God and biology, and to fly fast—for just one more moment—through the chill air and into the arms of the roaring crowd below. ⚡

SKI FEVER!

ALWAYS DOWNHILL, ALWAYS FASTER

BY CHARLIE MEYERS

Like most biological urges, the passion bursts forth in the early teens. Some say it is present at birth, a seminal urge lying dormant until it springs to life when mixed with snow. Whatever its genesis, this craving to ski uncommonly fast—deathly fast—is the emblem of the downhill racer, the ultimate risk taker in a sport full of them. It is a capricious siren, luring suitors to the brink, even past the brink, before bestowing either wealth or fame, or disaster.

In 1976, a farm boy named Franz Klammer danced that tightrope to an Olympic gold medal on a mountain above Innsbruck in his native Austria. From that moment, downhill racing, and the entire sport of skiing, was never the same. Driven by the frenzied urgings of his countrymen and his own raging ambition, Klammer courted calamity with every perilous turn in what veteran sportscaster Frank Gifford called the most exciting two minutes in the history of sport. Klammer, in the greatest season any skier ever experienced, won every downhill he entered, eight World Cup races and Olympic gold. He later admitted he'd been consumed by fear—not the fear of injury but the fear of falling.

The 1976 Olympic downhill, its riveting drama and international exposure, is considered by many to have been the signature event in the popularization of ski racing. Certainly it was the pivotal event in the lives of two North American racers who became symbols of downhill daring. In only his third year of international racing, but with a medal within his grasp, young Ken Read of Calgary shied away from the most direct line, perhaps the only fainthearted act of a ten-year career, and finished fifth. "I had discovered a very straight line early in training, one that I thought would allow me to win," Read recalls. "But then I fell, and when the race came, I didn't take it. After the race, journalist Serge Lang came to me and said, 'You backed off and Klammer didn't.' It was a lesson I never forgot." Driven, Read became leader of the Crazy Canucks, that wild band of Canadian downhillers who even today remain the inspiration of that nation's ski team. His five World Cup victories include the Hahnenkamm, the world's most demanding ski race.

Andy Mill was sixth at Innsbruck, just behind Read, but it was the uncommonly

This is the warrior class of skiing, men and women who regularly lunge into an encounter with gravity—that fickle element that can change suddenly from friend to foe. Those who do not recognize this split-second transformation often are carried away on their shields.

courageous way the Aspen skier achieved his placing that earned him a niche in the annals of the sport. On the first day of training, Mill took a brutal fall that left his lower left leg so bruised that he could not wear a ski boot for three days. His Olympic dream slipping away, Mill opted for a drastic and painful remedy. "I cut a piece of cardboard from a box and stuffed it into the back of my boot to distribute the pressure. Then, before the race, I sat down and packed snow around my leg to freeze it until just before it was time to run. There was no time for any kind of warm-up—just go. I was racing for more than just a medal. I was trying to get to the finish before my leg thawed."

Mill's feat ensured a lifelong reputation for audacity, as if a dozen years of reckless plunges down the mountains of the world were not enough. Mill's career ended in a 1981 crash at Wengen, Switzerland, in which he broke his neck and his back. "I walked to the helicopter thinking I had a kink in my neck," said Mill, who might be excused such underestimation since he'd previously survived two broken legs, a broken arm, a broken wrist, and eight major knee surgeries.

What untamed resolve drives someone to endure such peril? Read, a ski jumper in his youth, believes it's the same compulsion that propels an Indy driver to push his car to the threshhold of catastrophe. Mill, who raced motorcycles, thinks the urge for excitement springs from the womb. "You're born with a spirit either to climb on the monkey bars or to play in the sand," he says. "From the start, some have a kind of wildness that loves to challenge the limits, no matter what they may be." Tommy Moe, the 1994 Olympic downhill champion, spends his spare time kayaking raging Alaskan rivers.

Downhill and death are not far from one another. But never was the proximity so shocking as in the January 1994 crash at Garmisch-Partenkirchen, Germany, that took the life of Austria's Ulrike Maier. In few athletic endeavors are women placed at as much risk as in ski racing, often hurtling down treacherous slopes at speeds of up to seventy-five miles per hour. When a woman is killed, even this ice-edged sport is jolted. When the woman is a mother, as was Maier, the tragedy is compounded.

The sport mourned and then pushed on. Still downhill. Still faster.

You're born with a spirit either to climb on the monkey bars or to play in the sand. From the start, some have a kind of wildness that loves to challenge the limits, no matter what they may be.

Skiing is a sport that allows the physically challenged to enjoy the same thrills as mountain "normies". Today, nearly 10,000 participate in handicapped skiing in the U.S., either as recreation or competition.

SKI FEVER!

Speed skiing—Red-lining the mountain, no turns allowed. The first recorded speed-skiing event took place in 1880 in LaPorte, California. It was won by miner Tommy Todd, who clocked a blistering 87 mph on his trusty 12-foot 'longboards'. The record didn't improve much over the next 50 years. In 1931, during the first international event at St. Moritz, winner Leo Gasperl could only coax his boards to 85 mph. In following years, technology took off. The current record, 150 mph, was set by American Jeff Hamilton at Vars, France, in April, 1995. What you need to ski at terminal velocity-plus: boot fairings, low-friction suit, brain bucket, 240 cm skis…and a Passion for The Plunge.

Snowboarding, early an abbreviation of the teenage counterculture, has grown to capture adults and grizzled ski purists alike. And just like skiing, it's acquired its own specialists: racers, freestylers, and all-terrain freeriders.

There are probably no more extreme extremes in back-country skiing than skiing by helicopter or slogging through the puckerbrush under your own power. Bottom line: You work for it, or you pay for it.

But then, it doesn't much matter which way you earn it—freeheeling or fats. Exploring the raw, untamed world of the backcountry is unlike anything else in skiing. The backcountry skier gets the double whammy of skill-testing and discovery—discovery of self and of the wilderness that surrounds.

Silent, towering snow-laden conifers whisper to you as you glide among them—lodgepole, ponderosa, foxtail, bristlecone—the wind whistling through their branches. And those same branches shield the snow from sunlight, protecting it and keeping it in its untouched, pristine form just for you.

Backcountry

OPTIONS, ALTERNATIVES AND NOTIONS ON SKI ADVENTURING

BEAUTY AND THE BACKCOUNTRY

BY JEREMY SCHMIDT

It was almost dark by the time we topped the ridge and looked down into the broad snowy reaches of Boulder Basin. The sun had long since dropped from sight. The wind that had troubled us most of the day died to a whisper. Deep in the valley, a pool of shadow gathered and welled upward as the western sky went from pale orange to a warning shiver of violet—a forecast of intense cold.

A February night in the high Purcells might have felt intimidating except that 600 feet below us, at the edge of timber, sat a log cabin—windows glowing warmly from the light of gas lanterns, smoke rising gently from the stovepipe. An hour earlier, our friend Art had hurried ahead to light a fire and start supper, and after a day of cross-country skiing across the high snowfields we were all tired and hungry. But no one moved or spoke. The mountains had cast their ancient twilight spell, and we stood suspended between our eagerness to reach the cabin and the knowledge of how rare such moments are. Food could wait. In a few hours, this would be nothing more than a memory, but a lasting one. No one in our small group will ever forget the moment.

If I remember, it was not an easy trip. Worrisome avalanche conditions had forced us on a difficult, circuitous route. One of our party was a rank novice and was having a terrible time. My feet were cold, my back sweaty, my shoulders aching from the weight of my pack. We had eaten lunch among the crags, standing up against a punishing wind. Moments before arriving at the last ridge, I had wanted nothing more than to get my skis off and roast myself beside a warm fire.

Backcountry skiing does that to you—it lifts you up, then drops you hard. It takes you from the best to the worst and back again. I'm tempted to say that discomfort is one of the attractions of the backcountry, that hard-won rewards are the most deeply satisfying. Why else would you abandon the sophisticated, well-tuned delights of a ski resort? Why walk when you could ride a lift?

You see things in the backcountry that you don't see on groomed slopes—silent soaring peaks, deer, snowshoe hares, a marmot, eagle, or coyote, maybe even an elk or bighorn sheep—all those mountain creatures, big and small, that you only see in 'National Geographic' specials.

There are better reasons than pain. It feels good to venture into the wild heart of winter, a place where, by natural rights, we have no business surviving. Moose belong there, even chickadees. But humans, given our lack of fur and claws, should be migrators or hibernators. Without protective suits, we wouldn't last ten minutes. But we stay out in the worst weather for hours, even days. It gives us a wonderful sense of independence. True freedom is never having to say "uncle".

Especially at night. To be in the wilderness at night in the winter is a rare experience. When the moon is full, the snow gleams as if lit from within. On its brilliant surface—drawn perhaps by that brilliance—I have seen white snowshoe hares dance like deranged ghosts, silent and barely visible among the drifts. Mice and voles also appear from their burrows and run crazy zigzag paths. Owls are watching. So are ermines and coyotes and martens. If they had skis, I might understand why they do it. Skis are the greatest of all winter adaptations. They make us all a touch irrational, liable to perform inexplicable high-spirited acts. Without skis, we might as well head south with the geese, poor critters, equipped with only webs on their feet.

Instead, we climb mountains and ski the powder. I know of one particularly fine slope in northwest Wyoming that pushes up directly from the valley bottom for nearly 4,000 vertical feet of mixed glades and open meadows. It takes half a day to reach the top, depending on snow conditions and how many friends have come along to help break trail.

You climb to a mantra of creaking leather and steady breathing. Every twenty strides equals one turn on the way down. But no one counts. The valley recedes, the trees get smaller, the rocky crags grow nearer. Hitting the ridge, you stand around in celebration of the view, snap a few pictures, maybe eat lunch. There's no hurry, no sense of competition. Today you own this run. You can ski it right down the middle.

Skins are peeled off the skis and rolled into the pack. Transceivers are checked, zippers closed, drawstrings tightened, goggles snugged. And you're off. One turn, two, three, the rhythm is set, the snow billows into your face, your friends flank you on either side. There's a crazy hooting sound, and you realize it's your own voice.

There are dangers in the backcountry, but there is also reward. Prepare for it well, play by its rules, and the wilderness will charm and teach and mystify you. You just might become a 'liftline' dropout for life.

Each turn takes you in to your waist, only to rise again—ankle deep, thigh deep, ankle deep again—sending up a contrail thirty feet long. There's no hint of other ski tracks, not even beneath the surface where your skis rise and fall through the hissing softness. This is powder like a resort skier can only dream of. Out here the snow lies all winter tracked by nothing more than the occasional ptarmigan and red squirrel and groomed only by the weather. If you looked down, you wouldn't see your ski tips. You might as well look up and watch the clouds. Seeing isn't important. There are no obstacles. It's all feeling; it's all tactile, a matter of heart and soul. Consciousness centers, Zen-like, somewhere above the knees and below the head.

How many turns can you stand? Through an open glade, into the trees, out into a lower glade, over a big gentle roller, kissing the edge of a tree well, then a sharp drop and you're airborne, sideways, headed for catastrophe and giggling before the snow closes over your head.

As you lie there looking up at the blue alpine sky, skis akimbo, ice crystals from your explosive impact drift down, catching the sun and winking. It's a diamond day—turn it any direction, and it only looks better. ⚑

Miles from the nearest road, deep in the pure heart of winter, contemplating a vast panorama of snowbound peaks and, closer at hand, a snug place to spend the night with good friends. It's hard to imagine anything better.

HELI-HIGH

BY PETER OLIVER

You haven't truly felt your heart ballooning in your throat until you've flown over a knife-edged mountain ridge in a helicopter. Rising along one flank of the mountain toward the ridge, just a few feet above the rock and snow, surfing the lifting energy of thermal updrafts, you cross over the ridgeline, and the world suddenly falls away on the other side. In an instant, more than 1,000 feet of space disconnect you and terra firma. Imagine standing atop the world's tallest building and looking down to discover that the floor is gone. That's what it's like.

I'll bet plenty of helicopter pilots get a perverse charge out of executing ridgeline fly-overs when they know their cabins are filled with anxious, first-time heli-skiers. Let's introduce the uninitiated to that heart-rising feeling, let's prime their pumps. Then we'll set them down on a soft embankment of snow and watch them huddle in heli-skiing's rendition of a rugby scrum. And we'll let 'em have it with a mighty windblast of snow as the rotors of the chopper accelerate on liftoff. If you spend all day in the finest skiing environment in the world and never get to ski, how else are you going to amuse yourself?

It was Hans Gmoser, founder of Canadian Mountain Holidays, who came up with the grand idea in the mid-'60s that helicopters might make pretty good ski lifts in places where any other kind of ski lift would be untenable. It was Gmoser who scoped out the vast mountain wilderness of western Canada and, seeing a boundless expanse of ideal skiing terrain without lifts, put two and two together: helicopters and untracked powder in the wilderness.

But he has since wondered whether this grand idea was so grand after all. He wonders whether the thousands of heli-skiers who now visit western Canada every winter to immerse themselves in deep-powder nirvana really appreciate what makes heli-skiing special. Gmoser is a man, you see, who loves mountains. He loves their shapes and the ways their moods change with the weather and the seasons. He likes skiing, too—make no mistake about that—but he likes skiing primarily because it allows him to be in those mountains.

These days, heli-skiers seem to Gmoser to be obsessed with nonstop skiing in light, deep powder. They seem to cheat themselves, to miss out on the best part of the whole heli-skiing deal, which, says Gmoser, is "to get out in the mountains and enjoy the beauty."

"A few thousand feet of deep, untracked powder; the thrill of a long, fast descent; the exhausting exhilaration of a hundred or more linked turns—all of it is mesmerizing."

Well Okay, I'm willing to grant Gmoser that point. But, it is what we skiers live for—those moments of lightness in fresh powder snow. To pull ourselves away, even for a split second, is like trying to sober up on the spot.

I have also stood on the mountaintop, so to speak. I have looked around. I have taken time to admire the ways that nature has molded the earth's surface into those mountains that bring Hans Gmoser such contentment. I have tried to decipher the riddles of geology encoded in the rock spires, glacial cirques, avalanche paths, and river drainages that form the backdrop of your average heli-skiing run. I've tried to figure it all out. I've done my looking around, so I know what Gmoser is talking about. It is a rare view that helicopters provide—a view of mountains and snow and trees and glacial ice and blue skies. No signs of the crude, ill-considered things that humans do to the world in the name of civilization.

"Just the pure act of skiing—if this were all of it, I would be bored with it," Gmoser once confided to me. But after I've taken the time to appreciate my surroundings, I go skiing and love it. I enjoy the skiing and the looking around, equally as inseparable parts of a single experience.

Still, Gmoser makes sense, and maybe those ridge-skimming pilots aren't getting such a bad deal after all. Once they've had their fun scaring skiers, once they've windblasted the rugby scrum and have lifted off to be alone in the sky, they get to look around. They spend their time checking out possible landing spots, watching for indications of a change in the weather, noting the ways the snow has fallen or the wind has blown. They develop a personal relationship with the moods and angular details of the mountains while coming to terms with their extraordinary workplace.

So what if they aren't skiing? They're looking around. And Hans Gmoser would tell you that's the best part of the whole deal.

Mike Wiegle first came to B.C. from his native Austria as a twenty-year-old ski racer eager to see for himself the high mountains and deep snows that he'd heard and read about all of his life. In the thirty-five years since, Mike Wiegle Helicopter Skiing has grown into one the top heli-ski operations in North America. He has guided nearly 14,000 skiers through the Cariboo and Monashee Mountains of the Canadian Rockies.

FLIGHT OF THE WANNABE

BY JEANNIE PATTON

In a one-horse town that sits just below 10,000 feet in Colorado, a dozen friends gather in the steamy kitchen of a fellow cooking a deep vat of chunky potato soup and some homemade challah. He used to run a mountain inn but now hunkers down in dark winter with his happy chocolate lab and a quiver of backcountry skis. Annually, under the March full moon, we converge here for an extended run down 3,000 feet of Rocky Mountain stash. We know that to arrive at this edge of wonder, where we rely on equal parts balance, touch, finesse, and power, is to participate in a paradox. Each person's expertise braids into trace lines of snow that weave us—with each other and with the mountains—into a whole. "Work" selves and "play" selves unite; "out there" and "in here" merge in the same spirited place.

Our mixed bunch includes two serious mountaineers, half a dozen city folk, and three hard-core pinecone puppies who seldom drop below 8,000 feet for fear of attitude deterioration. We've been peering at a snarling sky for two days, wishing away the blustery storm. It's not that powder snow isn't welcome, but the helicopter pilot refuses to launch without starry skies, stable snow, and zero wind.

The snow keeps dumping, and we hole up in the two-story cabin, sleeping dorm-style in down bags. We spend the days fidgeting and running outside to cop an hour or three of backyard cruising up and down the couloirs and shoulders, poofing through holes in the ground-level clouds while the stainless-steel sky pours bucketloads of drifting flakes. We yelp in delight as snow with the toothsome texture of crystal sugar fluffs into our gaiters. Indoors, we cook hot sauces, eat, and watch for a break in the weather.

At ten o'clock on our second night, the wind shrinks to a snuffle and the snow lightens. We watch our pilot's face with the eagerness of whining retrievers. He nods, and we scatter to dress, to grab skis and poles, and to adjust packs. I layer polypro T-neck, fleece vest, jacket, and pants, pull on my headband, and stuff a ski cap into the pack. Avalanche transceivers are turned on, and ears strain to catch the small burps and beeps. We pack shovels and water, skins and snacks. We listen to walkie-talkie weather reports and hope that the gully walls won't shower us

in spindrift from late-season blowdowns. We know what we're about: these mountains are old friends. But every time is the first time.

I stand on the back deck and watch the first batch of four lift off from our foot-stomped helipad. The whump-whump-whump of the copter blade flattens and lifts spirals of snow as the magical machine lifts straight up in the air then arcs into the deep blue-black, pearl-tipped night.

The noise and commotion of the helicopter throws me into a state of exhilaration and trepidation, and I am breathless as we lift off next, and I watch the ground drop away in a flurry of blowing snowdevils. We ascend and then swing to the left to climb to the mountain's topmost ridge. There we gently alight on the packed snow. Crouching, we run from the eggshell bubble, hiding our faces from the copter's wild wash, eager for silence.

The first batch of skiers sits at the Etch-a-Sketch ridgeline, savoring the calm, clear quiet, the blue-light profiles of firs. No one hurries to leave the panorama of the Continental Divide, Arapaho Basin, Keystone's North Peak, the Ten-Mile Range, and the serrated edges of Gray's and Torrey's Peaks. The moon, only a sliver less than full, shines a fluorescent glow over the snow, and our eyes struggle to define shadows, rolls, mounds, and drop-offs in the dim light. This is the moment of truth.

We push off—first one, then another, and another. The tracks I'm following turn blurry blue, puffing steam envelopes the disappearing form in front of me. I adjust my goggles, tighten my pack, and drop off the ridge into sensual turns, slicing the icing in mock-eights of the perfect hourglass arcs that precede me. Exaggerate the motion. Reach for the turn. Swallow the holler and yelp—look forward and peer into the wispy face of God. 🎿

Skiing powder in the backcountry offers a litany of delights—the soft hiss of slivery turns and the gasping for breath in smoky waves of talc. The face shots and deep satisfaction of a gliding telemark turn. The absence of sound other than your own breath and the groan of trees. The launching of self into a weightless space with indefinite borders. The 'this is it-ness' of losing your perimeter and gaining the universe.

GEAR FOR GOING

BY JEREMY SCHMIDT

Backcountry is a broad term. It is any area beyond the reach of roads and grooming machines. It can be flat, gently rolling, or mountainous. It can be twenty miles into a wilderness area, or a quarter-mile from a busy highway. But conditions are wild and winter is always in charge. What do you need to stay safe and comfortable? That depends on what you want to do.

Beginning with skis, choices range from light touring to randonee. There is no perfect ski for all conditions. You balance your desire for control with the need to save weight. If all you do is climb for turns, wide boards with cable bindings are best. If you want to make miles, you'll prefer thinner and lighter skis.

Your boots should match your skis and your particular style. Some skiers, lighter on their feet, do well with less boot. Relying on finesse, they ski like surfers—riding their boards as much as controlling them. Others want cranking power, but they pay for it with extra weight.

Clothing is very much a personal choice. The trend is strongly toward synthetics and plenty of layers, including a loose-fitting, hooded wind parka and wind pants. One-piece suits are useful in extreme conditions at high altitudes and should have a full complement of zippers, vents, and pockets. You'll need glacier glasses, goggles, spare gloves or mittens, and sun cream.

In areas threatened by avalanche, everyone in the party should have a transceiver, a shovel, and a probe pole, and must know how to use them. Other items include a fire starter (a butane lighter and a candle work well), a headlamp, map, compass, spare food, and water.

Plan on camping? A good sleeping bag, sleeping pad, and tents are critical, unless you want to build a snow cave. The tent should be capable of standing up under a load of snow and should zip tight against blowing snow. It's very useful to carry a backpacking pressure cooker. This will allow you to cook inside your tent without generating steam. Otherwise, your stove will have to be outside.

Keep in mind that backcountry ski weather is not limited to winter. Spring touring can be best because days are long and warm and the snow is firm. During big snow years, the Sierras and Rockies are skiable well into June. In that case, pack beach chairs. ✦

"**K**eep in mind that backcountry ski weather is not limited to winter. Spring touring can be best because days are long and warm and the snow is firm."

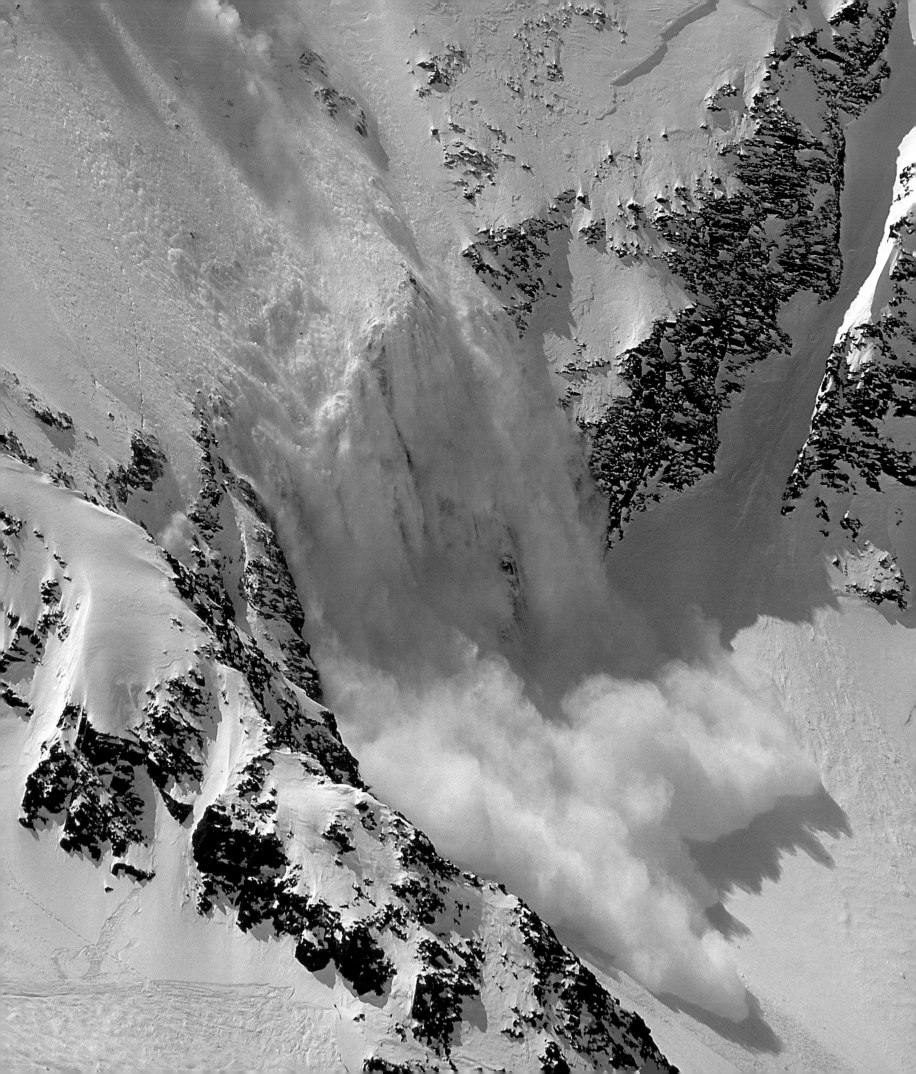

"Steep" is pretty much a state of mind. A slope that most skiers would label insane is nothing, after all, but a day of play for the extreme skier.

So is our mind—our perception of steepness—really all that different from that of an extreme skier? Peter Oliver makes the case that it isn't. It's a balancing act, he tells us, in which you weigh your physical and mental resources against "commitment." This is something he discovered at the top of a 2,000-foot couloir in Val d'Isere, France.

It's fun, if a bit intimidating, to be with Peter as he weighs his choices. It's also instructive to hear from Dan Egan, one of the world's premier skiers of extreme, who finds skiing the steeps "controlled chaos...but profoundly seductive."

For most of us, the impressions of these extreme skiers are as close to oh-my-God skiing as we'll ever get. And as David Goodman suggests, the biggest hurdle is, and always will be, making that first turn.

TheSteeps

COULOIRS, CLIFFS, GULLEYS—AND GUTS

THE FIRST TURN

BY DAVID GOODMAN

The first turn is always the hardest.

That time-tested cliché of the steeps taunted me as I stood paralyzed at the top of the forty-five-degree gully. Below me, a ribbon of white plunged 2,000 feet to the valley floor. The gully was hemmed in by rocky outcroppings and laced with ice bulges, making the sinewy corridor appear all the more menacing. But this was also a secret passageway through this forbidding landscape, an elegant line that tantalized and lured me. I stomped my skis into the firm snow, bent my knees, and shuffled my feet. But my mind overruled my legs; I couldn't budge. Minutes ticked away in slow, tortuous progression as I tried to talk myself into making a turn, but nothing succeeded in bringing me any closer to the bottom.

A several-hour hike up New Hampshire's Mount Washington had delivered me to this remote couloir. Mount Washington, the highest peak in the northeast, is the home of Tuckerman Ravine, a legendary proving ground of extreme skiing. Each year, I make a pilgrimage to the mountain, partly to pay my respects to this skiing shrine, partly to test myself once more on its fabled steeps. These journeys are a way to take my pulse as a skier, to see just how far I've come since the last time I was here. Some years, I push my limits. Other years, I am resoundingly humbled.

On this excursion, several friends and I had hiked to a little-known wilderness ravine on Mount Washington to claim a rarely skied backcountry prize: Airplane Gully, so named for a plane that once crashed here. Upon arriving at the top, my partners and I recoiled as we peered down the throat of the chute. The northwest-facing gully radiated a cold, steely glare, the frozen surface resisting the softening effects of the sun. After fifteen minutes of silent ogling, four of my five friends broke their numb stares, pulled back from the edge, and quietly rehitched their backpacks. "We're gonna go find something a little mellower," Peter announced, looking a bit shaken. They disappeared around a rocky knob and resumed their search for tamer terrain.

I flashed a look at Barry, my ski partner. "I'll ski it if you'll ski it," I proposed with a faint smile, privately hoping he would decline. Without hesitation, he nodded and snapped on his skis.

"**B**alancing precariously on the slender steel edges of my skis, my eyes looked on the route below. Stray too far left and I'd be forced onto the blue ice; too far right would suck me into a boulder field."

I slid slowly to the edge of the small cornice that overhung the top of the gully. Leaning over, I probed the snow to check its consistency. An inch of wet corn lay on top of a firm, granular base. It was skiable. I shifted forward, my skis sliced through the soft cornice, and I sideslipped onto the firm headwall of the gully. Then I stopped.

Balancing precariously on the slender steel edges of my skis, my eyes locked on the route below. The gully was shaped like an hourglass, narrowing sharply in the middle. Stray too far left, and I would be forced onto a bulge of dull blue ice; too far right would suck me into a boulder field. Directly below lay the passageway—a fifteen-foot-wide slot hemmed in by a house-sized boulder on one side and a rock wall on the other. All I had to do was link jump turns down the fall line, and the descent would be complete. I turned my shoulders down the hill, planted my pole hard in the snow, crouched like a tiger about to spring…and couldn't move.

Inside my head the mental chatter was deafening. "I'll hurtle uncontrollably into the rocks…The gully is too icy…It's steeper than it looks…I'm too old for this.…"

Fear is a constant partner on extreme terrain. It is a rational response to being in irrational places. The best skiers learn to harness the emotion. They control their fear, using it to sharpen all their senses and focus them on the task at hand. Me? I was just plain scared out of my wits.

I tried to staunch the flood of panicked thoughts. Closing my eyes, I visualized myself linking a perfect set of turns down the gully. My hips were swinging side to side; my skis were biting solidly into the snow; my poles were tapping like a jazz drummer beating a slow, perfect rhythm. Yes, I assured myself, I could do this. I planted my left pole hard and unweighted my skis.…

I opened my eyes to discover that I was still stuck like a fly to a wall. I couldn't move forward or back. My mind was mingling impassioned images of disaster with sensuous images of success.

A mixture of disgust, frustration, and terror coursed through my body. I finally tore my gaze from the gully and refocused on the surrounding peaks. A

Fear forces you to think—again and again—before proceeding. It is the mind's way of reminding you that the usual laws of gravity apply; you are not in Disneyland here.

crystal-clear blue sky framed the craggy, brilliant flanks of New Hampshire's White Mountains. The mountain ridges were a series of deep-blue waves that rolled off as far as I could see. This was a familiar place, one where I had learned many lessons over the years. I took in the panorama in deep, hungry gulps until it filled me up. Suddenly, I was a small speck in this natural universe, just one more creature flowing in the current.

My eyes gravitated back into the gully. It somehow looked different. I gazed far down the mountain, beyond where I could see. Fluidly and instinctively, my pole pierced the snow, my legs sprang skyward, and I took flight.

"**F**ear is a constant partner on extreme terrain. It is a rational response to being in irrational places. The best skiers learn to harness the emotion. They control their fear, using it to sharpen their senses and focus on the task at hand."

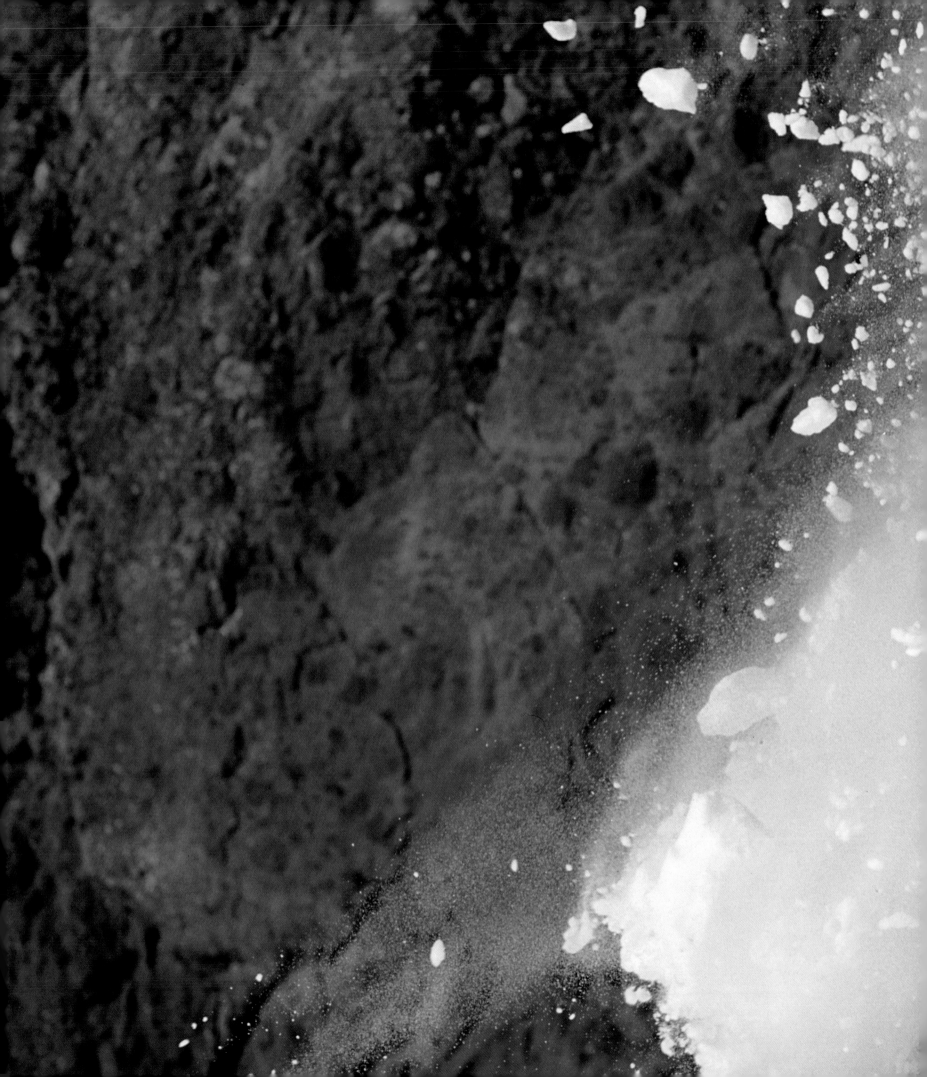

A STEEP STATE OF MIND

BY PETER OLIVER

How steep is steep? A friend tossed that question my way in the backcountry near Crystal Mountain, Washington, where we were assessing a slope we'd just skied. We were trying to calculate just how steep it really was—trying to figure out whether it qualified as one of the truly extreme, terrifyingly steep steeps of the world.

I hesitated in answering. I'm not good at making eyeball measurements of slope angles, and I'm not sure what the numbers really mean, anyway—those degrees and percentages that supposedly indicate steepness. And it occurred to me that maybe that wasn't the point. Steepness, I figured, isn't actually so much a matter of steepness as it is a state of mind. So I came up with this: It's steep if you think it's steep.

That didn't sit well with my partner, who snorted at my airy, imprecise answer. "If you ask me, that slope was friggin' steep, that's what I think," he said. Then he skied away, leaving me to wonder whether what I'd said was really as silly as he made it seem.

But I'll stick to my answer. I'll stick to the idea that steepness isn't really about slope angles. It isn't determined by finite measurements—thirty or forty or fifty degrees. Steepness is all in the mind; it's all about playing a head game with fear. The fact is, few slopes are true killer steeps, characterized by the disconcerting probability that if you fall, you die. But, in the play of the game, plenty of slopes can create that illusion.

I hold in high regard those skiers able to take on the most perilously steep slopes—the chutes of the Rockies, the couloirs of the Alps, the cirques of western Canada—with as little anxiety as a gardener plucking lettuce from a backyard plot. They know how to play the game of steeps, and they know it's not a physical thing. Graceful technique is not the key to skiing the most radical slopes. In fact, skiing extreme steeps can be, and often is, downright ugly skiing—traversing, backsliding, wide-footed turning. Due to the absolute necessity of survival, it can be remarkably slow.

The late Patrick Valencant, a legendary figure in the world of if-you-fall-you-die, was, as one of his partners once said, "not very pretty to watch" when descending a life-threatening

The game is on when you start thinking about what the slope can do to you rather than what you can do to the slope. For a novice, steepness can be anything with enough of a downhill slant to allow skis to slide; for extreme skiers, it extends to the physical limits of what a ski edge can adhere to.

couloir. Prettiness, in fact, is an incidental consideration when any small mistake can lead to death. What is appreciable in such skiing, if not necessarily visually spectacular, is a remarkable state of mind in action. A relaxed and unfazed concentration on a dangerous task. That is the unique gift of the masters of the steep.

All of us—you and I and even the likes of Patrick Vallencant—have to work our way up to new gradients of steepness through the same process. We attain confidence on certain pitches, rise to the next level and, once confident there, rise again to slopes that are steeper still until, at some point, we decide we've had enough. At that point, we know that we can't—or are unwilling to—go any steeper.

I would judge my steep state of mind to be much like that of most skiers. I don't go out of my way to terrify myself, and I'm willing to accept steepness only up to a point. My heart isn't aflame with a desire to sacrifice my life or parts of my body to the idiot pursuit of conquering something I don't stand a reasonable chance of surviving. But I do like being just a little bit scared. Being scared is part of being challenged, and being challenged is at the heart of the game of skiing steeps.

Now there is a critical moment in skiing any steep slope—the point of commitment. Summoning your mental and physical resources, feeling that premonitory adrenal rush of something intriguingly ominous, you decide to go for it. The game begins.

* * *

I was standing on the precipice of a 2,000-foot couloir in Val d'Isere, France. I would estimate the pitch, through my inadequate math, to have been somewhere around fifty degrees. The snow conditions, as the French might say, were *affreusse*, which is to say, awful. And just getting to that awful snow—weeks old and as chippy as old plasterboard—required rappelling by rope over a 100 foot icefall.

Had I been guided by my own good sense, I would have turned away from such stupidity. But I was in the company of a group of very good skiers and a crusty, heavy-smoking Alpine guide with an impressively aggressive idea of what can be considered skiable. In the battle between peer pressure and good judgment, peer pressure won out. It usually does.

But a funny thing happened. Once I realized I was committed to skiing this hellish wall of *neige affreusse*, a sense of calm took over. I looked down the couloir with relaxed clarity. I became utterly sure of the necessities of my mission—deciding where to turn and where to sideslip, the vital imperative of controlling speed, the importance of maintaining momentum, correctly judging the precise amount of edge pressure and angle to use, the whole ball of wax. And once I reached the bottom, where the pitch eased off in an alluvial fan of avalanche debris, I felt—if not the pleasurable rush I might feel skiing in, say, two feet of powder—a wonderful sense of accomplishment.

Then I turned to look back up the couloir as another man came tumbling down. He had made a critical error in allowing himself to traverse too far across the face of the couloir and ending up too close to the rock sidewall. He had no hope of making another turn, so he just toppled right over and slid on his back, at an alarming speed, for more than 1,000 feet, ending up with a broken leg.

He was a capable skier; he'd just played the mind game badly. At a critical point, he had been afraid to turn when he should have turned, and he had skied himself into an inescapable trap. A split second of fear leading to a bad decision; a small mental lapse.

When steepness gets to you—when it infiltrates your mind, makes you think unclearly, affects your judgment and your skiing—that's steep. ⛷

CONTROLLED CHAOS

BY DAN EGAN

There are two occurrences in nature that cause otherwise normal human beings who love skiing to behave in decidedly peculiar ways. The first of these natural occurrences is the topology of the planet earth, specifically those pointy things that reach toward the heavens. The second is the frozen form of precipitation that falls upon those earthly heights in a light, fluffy carpet.

Together these create what is known as steep and deep, the most formidable challenge known to alpine skiers: extreme skiing. Everything depends on edge control, body angulation, and the ability to react instantly to obstacles.

Truth be told, the steep and deep is controlled chaos: sliding snow, abrupt changes in the weather, and the ever-present challenge of staying balanced while remaining calm and strong. It's a crazy combination of everything you expect it to be—and more. Because of this, the steep and deep has driven many skiers to push themselves far beyond *their* physical and mental abilities.

The technical skier attracted to plunging down near-vertical descents in powder snow up to his waist, is mentally functioning at a level that the average skier can barely comprehend. It's a near-Zen experience: mind, body, and spirit must be functioning as one. Skiing radical terrain is a constant test of physical skills, and the skier must be utterly, completely focused.

The steep and deep is a realm that exists on the edge of fear, but it is no place for those who are afraid. While the extreme skier acknowledges fear as a healthy, valid emotion that inspires the survival instinct, to be afraid implies a lack of certainty that will threaten one's competence. Weighted with such doubt, it would be unwise to jump into that couloir.

The way to prepare to ski the truly steep is to be just that—prepared. And preparations begin long before you stand on top of a cornice. Extreme skiers study and memorize their routes through the steep and narrow. Snow pits are dug out to calculate the avalanche danger. Escape routes are thought through. Islands of safety—rocks to hide behind in case of avalanche—are sought and identified. Every extreme skier atop a couloir understands that the first turn must be perfect, for it sets the rhythm for the rest of the run. Once the commitment has been made and the action begun, instinct takes over, senses heighten, and the entire universe shrinks down to the width of the couloir. A successful run is one you walk away from.

The steep and deep is profoundly seductive to skiers, wild and delectable but also dangerous. You must be a calculated risk taker to ski it, reassessing the terrain and snow conditions moment by moment.

"**O**nce the commitment has been made, instinct takes over, senses heighten, and the entire universe shrinks to the width of the couloir. A successful run is one you walk away from."

Respect the steep—it holds adventure and mystery. Engage in this activity and feel your soul merge with your body and mind. Ski it and treasure what you find, in the snow and in yourself.

Skiing didn't begin in North America. It began, as history records it, in Finland nearly 5,000 years ago. At that time, skis were used for hunting, transportation, and waging wars. Fifty centuries later, the Austrians—with a little help from the Swiss and the Brits—turned the ski into an elegant sporting tool and exported it for all the world to ogle. And ogle it Americans did, as we embraced the culture, traditions, and personalities of the sport.

Mostly the personalities. Lucky for us, they embraced the skiing lifestyle and determined that it was good for us. As Nicholas Howe explains, we have these visionaries to thank—for The Fever.

MakingTracks
TRADITIONS, TRIALS AND LEGACIES

THE BOYS WHO INVENTED WINTER
by Nick Howe

THE BOYS WHO INVENTED WINTER

BY NICHOLAS HOWE

People didn't used to go outdoors in winter, not if they could help it. That's what civilization was all about—we hadn't spent all those years getting from a cave to the downtown club with a bottle of sherry at the hearthside only to go outdoors again. And mountains? Well, mountains were a piece of bad luck for travelers and farmers.

Then, during the long optimistic summers of Queen Victoria's reign, when British gentlemen took lodgings in remote alpine villages such as Grindelwald and Chamonix and, as they would say, assayed the heights, mountains were incorporated into civilization. In 1864, four Englishmen were finishing up the summer season in St. Moritz. As they gathered in the Engadine Lounge of the Kulm Hotel to say goodbye to Joseph Badrutt, the proprietor, he enthusiastically described the fine winter weather in St. Moritz and the healthfulness of winter life there. The novelty of the notion appealed to the gambling spirit of the four gentlemen who'd been convinced that their London club provided all the relief they needed from the dismal London winter. Sensing an opening, Herr Badrutt bet them free lodging that a winter in St. Moritz was better than a winter in London. If a moment is needed to mark the beginning of winter resort life, that was it.

In 1905, Melvil Dewey, creator of the Dewey decimal system of classification, among other things, was overtaken by a vision so eccentric that it became irresistible: he decided to keep his club—The Lake Placid Club in upstate New York—open for the winter. He and his son Godfrey, along with four men, five women, and one child, spent the winter in the great Adirondack wilderness. When spring came they were still alive, and the encouraged Melvil ordered forty pairs of skis from Norway. The skis arrived soon after with leather toe straps and one pole per pair, as clumsy a rig as any donned by a rusticating city fellow. Because the only idea of winter sports that people had at the time (beyond billiards) was tobogganing.

Henry van Hoevenberg built a toboggan run on a nearby mountain. In their spring report, club officials reported on their success: "People almost literally had to be taught how to enjoy winter." The Lake Placid Club hired its first ski instructor in 1922 and became the first American resort devoted to winter sports.

Ten years later, Godfrey Dewey almost single-handedly engineered a successful bid for the 1932 Olympic Winter Games, the first in the western hemisphere. But the idea had not originally met with unanimous acceptance. At first, and naturally, too, many residents were aghast. And rightly so—the first bobsled team to practice came over the top of the last curve and toppled an outhouse, occupied at the time. Nevertheless, the Talon Hookless Fastener Company ran an ad for the Winter Olympics featuring a trim and prominently zippered young lady holding a golf club, radio linkups carried news of the Olympics to areas as far away as Georgia, and Lake Placid became a fixture in America's winter imagination.

 owell Thomas, lifelong ski promoter and world-renowned broadcaster, reporting from the Green Mountain Inn in Stowe, Vermont, in one of the nightly news shows he broadcast from ski area base lodges.

* * *

Another hand was at work developing the promise of winter. New York financier Averell Harriman, to the manor born and a devoted skier, had developed a taste for mountain vigor while on well-couched tours of Europe. He'd also developed a taste for the accumulation of money. By the mid-1930s, when he was chairman of the board of the Union Pacific Railroad, rival railroads were leading southwest and trolling for wealthy winter vacationers with such catchy lines as, "Go To The Sun Through The Sun" and "Go Where The Sun Spends The Winter." Harriman's trains led to the dimly lit northwest and carried mostly sheep and cattle, who had cheap tickets and few vacation plans.

Harriman commissioned an Austrian skiing friend, Count Felix Schaffgotsch, to find a place served by his railroad where he could build a St. Moritz in America. The Count searched until, on the point of giving up, he accidentally came upon a small railhead town best known for sheep and the legend that Jack Dempsey had been knocked down in a local barroom fight. A mile up the road was a large ranch for sale surrounded by treeless slopes. The town was Ketchum, a not unpromising name, and Harriman came out to tour the valley in an old-fashioned covered wagon heated by a pot-bellied stove. He was accompanied by William S. Paley, chairman of the board of CBS, and together they decided that this was the spot.

In the next few months, a bravura combination of wisdom and shrewdness were displayed. Mindful of the delicate constitutions of modern Americans, the builders asked the former owner of the ranch where his cattle had gathered on the coldest days. That would be the warmest place on the spread— and Harriman built his hotel exactly there. The Union Pacific spent $1.5 million on the hotel, and it was an astonishing building. The marble for the bathrooms was quarried in Italy, and the dining room entrance, the focus of the fan-shaped floor plan, led to carpeted steps bounded by velvet ropes on copper stanchions. The stairway faced west, and arriving guests were bathed in golden sunlight from the opposite windows.

But all this was being done in an attempt to develop a sport that few Americans knew how to play, in a town nobody had ever heard of, in a state many couldn't find on a map. So Harriman hired Steve Hannagan, whose previous job had been selling a desolate wasteland in Florida, which he'd subsequently named Miami Beach. By now, Harriman's own beguiling fantasy had been named Sun Valley, catching a memorable ring off his rivals' advertising.

Hannagan went to work. Johnny Weissmuller, who'd won a hatful of gold medals in Olympic swimming, was now at the height of his popularity as Hollywood's Tarzan. Hannagan hired a look-alike model and had him photographed stripped to the waist and glistening with suntan oil, posed on skis atop a pile of white gypsum. It was all there: sun, snow, skiing, and the great hero of warm-weather sports and far-off, exotic places.

In those days, skiing was largely a matter of rucksack and climbing skins: Hike up in the morning, have a sandwich for lunch, and ski down in the afternoon. No such pedestrian effort at Sun Valley. The Union Pacific engineers were asked to find a way to let skiers climb the mountain sitting down. Jim Curran, the man in charge, had worked with an endless-cable banana loader, so they gathered in the freight yard at Omaha as he hung a chair from a cable. Harriman asked his friend, financier J.P. Morgan, to try the chair, which he did, advising Harriman to go with it. The first chairlift was on Dollar Mountain, but Harriman soon added a second on Ruud Mountain at a cost of $185,000. Fearing a

Ski lifts of one form or another have been around for over a century. But it was in the 1930s that uphill conveyances were first given serious thought, leading to the development of the rope-tow in 1932 and the J-bar in 1935. Development of Jim Curran's chairlift at Sun Valley (pictured far left) was followed by the aerial tramway in 1938 and the T-bar in 1940.

public outcry at the obvious dangers of the venture, Harriman called at first for the chairlift to run at a stately four feet per minute.

The grand opening party for Harriman's hotel was December 21, 1936. Mr. Pullman of train fame was present as were Mr. Otis of elevators, and Mr. Fleishman of yeast and gin. As the festivities gained momentum, Hollywood producer David O. Selznick, actor Erroll Flynn, and a Chicago banker had a fistfight over the dance floor favors of actress Claudette Colbert. With entertainment like that, it hardly mattered that there wasn't any snow. It was only after the snow did come, six days later, that the management realized that they'd neglected to cut the brush from the ski slopes.

Harriman's improbable dream prospered beyond all expectations, and while the fledgling sport struggled to its feet among the logging roads and clapboard farmhouses of New England, chefs at Sun Valley were writing menus in four languages and fresh flowers greeted early risers on the coldest winter days. Sun Valley became the very soul and image of the destination resort—there was nothing beyond it.

* * *

In 1936, Pete Seibert's parents could not have booked tickets to Sun Valley. Like many Americans, they were just trying to hang on through the Great Depression. Seeking a better chance, they moved from south of Boston to the valley below Mount Washington, in the White Mountains of New Hampshire. There was some skiing up there, and young Pete liked to look through *Ski Annual*, the only American publication devoted to the sport. A page in the 1936 issue made a powerful impression on him. One photograph showed St. Anton, a tiny Austrian town, the wide eaves of the houses laden with snow, the mountains soaring in the background. Another showed Hannes Schneider, who had opened a ski school in St. Anton in 1907. Three of Schneider's instructors came to teach at ski schools near the Seibert's house in New Hampshire in the1930s, and in 1939 Schneider himself arrived in North Conway. Pete was one of the children making an arch of ski poles under which the Schneiders walked when they arrived.

During the Second World War, Seibert joined many other skiers in the Tenth Mountain Division. On training bivouacs in the Rocky Mountains, he searched for a place to build a ski resort

Pete Seibert was a Tenth Mountain Division veteran of the Second World Warl who bought an old ranch in Vail Pass, Colorado, in 1957, founding one of the most enduring and popular ski resorts in the country.

after the war. Many of the Tenth Mountain troopers dreamed of making a living skiing, but skiing held about the same place in the American imagination as polo—only a few rich people did it. Besides, skiers already had Stowe and Sun Valley, what more would they need? But Seibert continued to dream of his own ski area.

After the war, despite having been wounded in Italy, Seibert made the 1950 FIS World Championship team for the Aspen races and stayed on to teach in the ski school. Aspen had flared during the nineteenth century, a supernova in the silver boom. When silver was demonetized in 1893, miners left town so fast some didn't even clean out their closets. In 1940, the same spirit of hopeless odds that animated those prospectors had inspired the few remaining residents to successfully bid on the national alpine championships even though they had neither slope nor lift.

In the winter of 1957, Seibert was still looking for a spot that matched his dreams when a friend told him about an old ranch that was for sale west of Vail Pass. From the mountaintop above the ranch, looking at the bowls and ridges all around him, Seibert knew this was it.

* * *

Back east, in 1947, another veteran had opened Mohawk Mountain in Connecticut. He was tall and raw-boned, with a fire in his eye and a crew-cut that could remove paint. Brilliant, erratic, iconoclastic, Walt Schoenknecht was the man who would put the masses on skis.

Mohawk had 640 feet of vertical slope and not much snow, so Schoenknecht found a way to make his own—a sort of winterized lawn sprinkler. Venturi physics were not fully explored, and his device had a supersonic byproduct, which brought howls from every dog for miles around, but by 1949, Schoenknecht had America's first snowmakers at work, and before long, Mohawk was the largest rope-tow ski area in the world.

Eager to widen his net, Schoenknecht crossed North America seven times, and even studied Japan in search of the largest mountain nearest the most people. He settled on Mount Pisgah, behind Ruben Snow's old farm in southern Vermont. Schoenknecht had thought of

The U.S. ski racing team (Left) at the 1950 FIS Alpine World Championship in Aspen, Colorado. Left to right: Toni Matt, Leon Goodman, Dean Perkins, Gale Spence, Jack Reddish, Dave Lawrence, Coach Barney McLean, Pete Seibert, Dick Movitz, Steve Knowlton, and Jim Griffiths.

naming Mohawk "Mount Snow" after his snowmakers but decided it was too corny. Now he couldn't resist, although perhaps he should have stuck with Pisgah—that was the name of the mountain from which Moses saw the Promised Land.

Not sure he had enough mountain, Schoenknecht invited high-level people in Washington to set off an atomic bomb on Mount Snow, which he hoped would pile up enough earth to shape the extra terrain he wanted. When his invitation was declined, Schoenknecht turned his restless imagination to the bottom of his dream.

The floors of base lodges were always a problem—all slush and mud. Schoenknecht made the floor of his cafeteria out of pea stone, with drains underneath. The state inspectors took one look and said, "Walt, this is crazy—you can't have a dirt floor in a restaurant." The next day, Schoenknecht called them back to say he'd fixed the problem. The inspectors were skeptical, certain that he couldn't possibly have rebuilt the floor overnight. They came anyway, only to find the same gravel floor. But Schoenknecht was quick to point out the narrow new floor along the food line, and a sign with two arrows. The arrow pointing to the narrow strip of floor leading to the food said "Cafeteria;" the other, pointing toward the tables on the gravel, said "Picnic Area." Schoenknecht insisted on seeing the regulation forbidding an indoor picnic area. No such regulation could be found.

Schoenknecht went through seventeen chairlift designs before coming up with one of the most improbable of all. He'd taken the idea from an auto assembly plant in Deerborn, Michigan: chairs hung on chains hung from pulleys laced into steel I-beams. They were very slow and very low, but there was a method to his madness: The lifts were calculated to reassure beginners. And if trouble did come, the lifts could be evacuated with a stepladder. The I-beams were welded together end-to-end, and with no relief points in the system, the vibration built up fast. Copious applications of grease helped, but it also dripped onto passengers, so a tin roof was erected above each chair.

The hotel program shared the same give-it-a-try attitude. Despite a broken leg at the time, Schoenknecht hopped around in his cast. Drawing an X in the dirt with his crutch, he said, "Okay, that's one corner." Looking up at the mountain and looking around at the terrain, he hopped some more and then drew another X—"Okay, that's another corner."

Skiers prepare to hit the slopes at Mount Snow, in the early sixties. Note the cable bindings (Left), Cubco bindings (Center) and lace ski boots.

Schoenknecht's army duty in Japan had made a deep impression on him and its influence showed in his shrubbery plantings, in the pagodalike horizontals of the architecture, and in the water. There was water everywhere: the base lake, the inn lake, the Japanese Dream Pools, the goldfish tanks used for room dividers. His most elegant restaurant had a sort of jungle in it, with an occasional frog jumping out to greet diners. There was an outdoor swimming pool and the highest fountain in Vermont, the United States, or the world. It created such an immense pile of ice that Schoenknecht named it Fountain Mountain, put a Poma lift on it, and had ski races in July.

As Schoenknecht saw it, he wasn't merely competing with other ski areas but with the whole tradition of winter vacations in warm places. Thus the startled natives of Vermont saw America's first systematic effort to merchandise skiing to nonskiers: There were horses and snowmobiles, there were indoor skating and outdoor swimming with a fifteen-foot glass wall to focus solar warmth. Schoenknecht's was a pioneering theme park of winter entertainment. He had ideas about the skiing, too: "It doesn't matter if you have one trail or fifty, if they're all the same, it's boring." Denied the services of a nuclear explosion, Schoenknecht contoured his trails with banked turns and unusual saucer constructions.

Mount Snow's was not the smoothest opening a resort ever had. The roads were so bad that skiers rode in on logging trucks courtesy of the resort. And when the base lodge bathrooms became overcrowded during the first Christmas week, Schoenknecht handled it with typical originality—he turned the heat off to speed up the turnover.

Once in business, Schoenknecht thought numbers. He figured that on a good day they were handling more people than the lower level of Grand Central Station. When nearby Pine Top had 300 skiers, Snow had closer to 10,000. The tickets were within reach of almost everyone: Seven days, lodging, meals, lift, and ski school cost $57.95. There were five inns nearby, and 119 more would open in the next ten years.

But something beyond facilities and terrain was at work. Without realizing it, Schoenknecht was poised on the wave of the future. Generations of skiers had struggled with lace-up boots. Now the buckle-closure Henke Speedfit debuted with an unforgettable pitch: "Are

his claim map and soon McCoy was staking his own claim, starting from scratch, building Mammoth one lift at a time— he even made the clutches and gear boxes for the lifts. Today, McCoy's handiwork is a world-wide benchmark.

McCoy also launched another great work. Working as a soda jerk in Independence, he met a pretty Bishop cheerleader. Her name was Roma, and that was that. Together, they had six children and, soon, a very extended family of skiers in the race program. At one point 50 percent of the U.S. men's ski team and 100 percent of the women's team trained at Mammoth, including four McCoys.

Today, McCoy's extended family has grown from 300 to 25,000 on a good day on the mountain.

you still lacing while others are racing?" After ages of wooden skis, metal Heads and Harts were all the rage; after uncounted tons of plaster for sprained ankles and broken legs, Marker and Cubco "safety" bindings were everywhere. Ever since the war ended, skiers had worn baggy drab olive outfits from army surplus stores, while the more stylish wore dark-gray pleated gabardines. Now Bogner stretch pants in a rainbow of colors lit up the slopes. Doctrinal wars swept through American ski schools, and even the human body was seen in a new light; an article in *The Atlantic Monthly* advanced a startling thesis: "Exercise Does Keep Weight Down." Bonnie Prudden, the first great fitness guru, set up shop at Mount Snow. The hardy denizens of winter, raised in the age of rucksack and climbing skins, stood slack-jawed in amazement. The ultimate benediction came when *Life Magazine* visited Mount Snow in January 1959. The masses came to ski then in unimagined numbers, and the future was almost complete.

Schoenknecht was always a mass of conflicting impulses. He had his crews straighten salvaged nails to be reused, while spending the money to heat both the pool diving board and the concrete surrounding the pool: ninety-five degrees at poolside; seventy-five at the far edge. At the time, oil cost just thirteen cents a gallon, but then the Arab embargo struck. Foreclosures and receiverships followed. Schoenknecht himself was eventually forced out but kept rooms at Mount Snow until the day the new managers piled all his clothes in the parking lot. The beautiful servant returned to Mohawk then, to tinker with a conveyor belt for skiers.

Schoenknecht is gone now, most of the great originals are. Today, news of a ski resort is often buried in a back chapter of some global investment company's annual report, a place where improbable ideas are at a low premium. The sheep are gone from the old ranches, and the dogs no longer howl when the snowmakers are turned on in the night. But skiers should never forget the boys who invented winter. ⚡

Stein Erikson (opposite), 1952 Olympic gold medalist, shows the fast, graceful style at the 1950 FIS Alpine World Championships in Aspen that would later earn the expatriate Norwegian the adoration of American skiers. In the sixties, skiing's rally cry was "Ski like Stein!"

BY KURT MILLER

Skiing and filmmaking, to me, have always had a lot in common. Each is a means of personal, individual expression. Each, in its purest sense, is freedom. And while one delivers it, the other captures it, preserving and enhancing it so that others can experience it as well.

My own first taste of freedom, the genuine kind when you just seem to boldly, blindly soar, came to me as a child. I don't remember how old I was—four, maybe five—but I do remember what I was doing. I was skiing. It was at Sun Valley, and I was with my family during our Christmas powwow, which was to become an annual Miller tradition. Today, we still ski together, though sometimes at different times and places. And our family has grown.

FamilyFilms

FROZEN MOMENTS, BIG-SCREEN ACTION, AND THE SKIING LIFESTYLE

The experiences—the lessons—never change. You can ski together no matter what the differences in ability, and your son or daughter skis as well as you do for exactly one day of your life.

Skiing means friends and family, but more important, it's an individual sport. There's no pressure to compete, no pressure to carry the ball for the team, no pressure to perform for others. I was raised on the beaches of California, surfing and sailing—sports, like skiing, where you're responsible for yourself, where there are no boundaries and how far you go is up to you. Skiing is all that and—I return to the word—freedom. That freedom became, and will always remain, my fever.

Growing up in a filmmaking family taught me several things about skiing. Skiing—with its beauty, drama, grace and its rhythms—lends itself to film better than any other sport. Skiing is also something you can portray and enjoy on film, wherever you or your subjects are in life— with a love, a spouse, kids or grandkids—and it allows all of you to enjoy the trip, the ride, the experience, at the same level.

Technologically, there have been some interesting parallels in skiing and filmmaking. The breakthroughs in skiing—in snow grooming, in equipment, and skiwear—have made the sport safer, easier, warmer, and a lot more enjoyable. The same can be said of filmmaking. Fifteen years ago, home video wasn't available. Today, filmmaking has advanced from film to video to laser disk to digitized images that can be displayed full-screen on your home computer.

It has elevated the art of outdoor adventure films, of which Warren Miller's films have been an integral and important contribution. Warren's vision, like that of Walt Disney, is to entertain. To this day, that remains our goal and committment—to bring enjoyment to our audience by portraying the thrills and drama of real-life outdoor adventure.

In this book, we have gathered the most spectacular images and best writers in skiing to express the freedom and beauty this spectacular sport has to offer.

This reflects not only the spirit of skiing but the spirit of Warren Miller's films.

As long as skiing continues to thrive—and who doubts that it will?—we will continue to develop better ways to portray its spirit. And as long as it continues to inspire great images and great writing, and to draw out the emotions of those people able to deliver them, the literature of the sport will thrive as well.

Catch the Ski Fever!

Photo Credits

Per Breiehagen: 85.
David Brownell: 21, 24, 88 & 89.
Margaret Durrance: 142, 143, 148, 149, 154.
Ken Gallard: 25, 28, 47.
Mark Gallup: 4 & 5, 44, 75, 106, 122, 131, 141, 157.
Mark Gallup/RAP Films: 52, 86 & 87, 91, 94, 114, 128.
James Kay: 32 & 33, 92 & 93, 160 .
Mammoth Ski Resort: 153.
Scott Markewitz: front cover, 8 & 9, 16, 17, 18, 22, 34, 35, 39, 42, 45, 48, 53, 65, 107, 127, 132 & 133, 135, 136, 138, 156.
Scott Markewitz/RAP Films: 12, 108, 118, 140,
Mt. Snow: 13, 15, 147a & b, 150.
Lori Adamski-Peek: 36, 54, 66, 162 & 163, 164.
Larry Prosor: 1, 2 & 3, 6 & 7, 26 & 27, 30 & 31, 43, 51, 71, 76, 77, 81, 96, 103, 105, 109, 111, 112 & 113, 115, 119, 120 & 121, 123, 124 & 125, 137, 139, 159, 165, 166 & 167.
Alec Pytlowany: 57, 60, 68 & 69, 78 & 79, 80, 98 & 99, 101.
Neal Rogers: 37, 97, 102, back cover.
Sports File: 55, 58, 61, 62 & 63, 64, 72 & 73, 74.
David Stoecklein: 19, 23, 29, 40 & 41, 82 & 83, 84, 116 & 117, 161.
Stowe Ski Resort: 145.
Sun Valley Ski Resort: 144, 146.

Richard Needham's love affair with skiing began at the age of 18 in Caberfae, Michigan. Since then, he has skied more than ninety areas in fourteen countries, authored two books (*SKI's Encyclopedia of Skiing, Ski: Fifty Years in North America*), hosted two radio series (Ski Spot, On the Slopes), and is a recipient of the Lowell Thomas Award for excellence in ski journalism. The former editor-in-chief of *SKI Magazine*, Needham still writes of his skiing experiences—his ski fever—as *SKI Magazine's* editor-at-large.

Dan Egan is a world-renowned extreme skier and award-winning film producer. A member of the elite North Face Extreme Team, he and his brother John have skied the most remote regions of the world. He is a veteran of eleven Warren Miller ski movies and executive director of Ski 93, a consortium of four New Hampshire ski areas. Dan lives with his wife, Mihaela Fera, a three-time Olympic skier from Romania, near Franconia Notch, New Hampshire.

David Goodman is a contributing editor to *SKI, Powder,* and *Backcountry* magazines. His articles have also appeared in *Outside, Travel & Leisure, Men's Journal* and other publications. His book, *Classic Backcountry Skiing: A Guide To The Best Ski Tours* in New England was awarded the North American Ski Journalists Association's Harold S. Hirsch Award for Excellence in Ski Book Writing, as well as the Ullr Award from the International Ski History Association. Goodman is also a two-time recipient of the Harold S. Hirsch Award for Excellence in Ski Magazine Writing. He lives with his wife and daughter near Stowe, Vermont.

Paul Hochman is a contributing editor to *SKI Magazine*. He has also been a member of *SKI's* ski test team since 1991 and was a three-year member of the Dartmouth Men's Ski Team. Hochman is also a frequent contributor to *Men's Journal* and to *GQ* and writes a monthly column in *Dunkshot*, a Japanese magazine covering the NBA. His work has appeared in *The Sunday New York Times Magazine, HG, The Philadelphia Inquirer* and other publications. Hochman lives in Telluride, Colorado with his wife, Tricia, and his daughter, Lily.

Nicholas Howe lives in Jackson, N.H., one of the cradles of American skiing. His family opened a ski lodge in Jackson in 1933, a time when skiing was a word-of-mouth affair on lumber roads and farmers' pastures, so small a sport that most American practitioners knew each other by sight. Then in December 1936 the epochal Hannes Schneider Ski School of St. Anton opened a branch in an apple orchard just down the road from the Howes' place and 16 years later Nick was working at Sun Valley in the company of Stein Eriksen, Christian Pravda, and the iron of the U.S. ski team. This led, indirectly, to a career in journalism largely but not exclusively concerned with skiing. He has written nearly 2,000 articles for magazines, newspapers, television, and radio, he was the media liaison for the U.S. women's alpine team in 1981-88, and his work has appeared in a number of anthologies published in America and Europe. His knees are still intact after 55 years on skis, but he has the unique and unwelcome distinction of having been hit by both the Soviet KGB and Red Brigade terrorists while working in ski country.

Charlie Meyers is the ski editor of the *Denver Post* and a contributing editor to *SKI Magazine*. He has seen every downhill champion, from Jean-Claude Killy to Picabo Street, in the course of 29 years of World Cup watching. He has been selected as the nation's top ski writer four times and is a two-time winner of the Lowell Thomas Award.

Kurt Miller is the co-owner of Warren Miller Entertainment with his partner Peter Speek. Kurt grew up in Southern California and is a three-time All-American and World Class sailor. Since he became involved with the company, Kurt has created and developed a number of unique entertainment and sponsorship components which have added to the successful Warren Miller film tour. Projects have included *Ski World* magazine, Warren Miller Television, as well as ventures in both CD-ROM and book publishing. Today, Kurt shares responsibilities with Peter Speek in producing and directing the annual feature ski film and all Warren Miller Entertainment productions.

Ever since **Warren Miller** spent three and a half months in 1946 living in the Sun Valley parking lot, and spending less than twenty dollars doing it, it has been *downhill* all the way. Warren has learned to ski, run a movie camera, raise three children and produce over four hundred movies. Today the Warren Miller annual feature length ski film marks the beginning of the ski season in cities all around the world. His off beat humor has earned him a guest spot on countless TV talk shows, and a successful career as a film producer, writer and cartoonist.

Peter Oliver's enthusiasm for skiing has carried him to more than ninety ski areas of the world from the Rockies to the Alps, Vermont to Australia. His dream run goes like this: two feet of powder on a windless, sunny day; a thirty-degree slope without avalanche worries; the company of good friends; and a bottle of Cabernet in a rucksack. He is a contributing editor for *Skiing Magazine* and is the author of, among other books, *The Insider's Guide To The Best Skiing in New England*.

Colorado native **Jeannie Patton** remembers the first time she camped out at age thirteen, and she's barely come indoors since. A former river guide and rock climbing instructor, she is an avid skier who currently teaches college English in Boulder. As a contributing editor for *SKI Magazine*, she won the Lowell Thomas Award for a feature article on Vail. Her work has also been published in *Skiing, Powder, Snow Country*, and *Outside* among other national magazines. In the summer of 1994, Jeannie walked 500 miles from Denver to Durango and is now working on a book about her trek.

Jeremy Schmidt has lived in the Rocky Mountain west for 15 years. When first coming to the area, he had worked at a variety of jobs: park ranger, winterkeeper, wilderness guide, ski instructor and teacher. Since 1977, he has been a full-time writer and photographer with a special interests in wilderness, natural history, and adventure. Most of his work is for magazines and recently numerous books. Credits for magazine feature stories include *Audubon, Outside, International Wildlife, Adventure Travel, Arizona Highways, Harrowsmith, Powder, Reader's Digest, Ski Canada*, and others. Jeremys' most important magazine work has been for *Equinox*, a Canadian science and geography magazine. Assignments for them have taken him to Africa, Russia, New Zealand, Tibet, China, Thailand, Mexico, and many points in Canada. Having returned from a nine-month journey circling the Himalayas sponsored by Camden House, the book division of *Equinox*, he authored a travel narrative tentatively titled *Dreams of High Mountains*. Other books include travel guides, *Adventuring in the Rockies* (Sierra Club, 1987) and a small natural history guide, *Lehman Caves* (Great Basin National Park, 1987).

Lito Tejada-Flores has spent the last twenty-nine years researching the pleasures and patterns of powder skiing. He's taught skiing in four languages, on two continents, and is the author of *Breakthrough on Skis: How To Get Out of the Intermediate Rut*, a book and video that have become modern classics. Lito lives in Crestone, Colorado, beneath the highest summits of the Sangre de Cristo range.